Session Notebook

INFORMATION

Name ————————————————

Phone ————————————————

Email ————————————————

Session Notebook

Date: Start Time: Session No:

Client Name: Session Time:

Topic:

Session Taking Points	Key Points From Previous Session

Notes: _____

_____

_____

_____

_____

_____

_____

_____

_____

_____

_____

_____

_____

_____

_____

_____

_____

_____

_____

_____

Session Notebook

Date: Start Time: Session No:

Client Name: Session Time:

Topic:

Session Taking Points	Key Points From Previous Session

Notes: _____

_____

_____

_____

_____

_____

_____

_____

_____

_____

_____

_____

_____

_____

_____

_____

_____

_____

_____

_____

Session Notebook

Date: Start Time: Session No:

Client Name: Session Time:

Topic:

Session Taking Points	Key Points From Previous Session

Notes: _____
_____
_____
_____
_____
_____
_____
_____
_____
_____
_____
_____
_____
_____
_____
_____
_____
_____
_____
_____

Session Notebook

Date: Start Time: Session No:

Client Name: Session Time:

Topic:

Session Taking Points	Key Points From Previous Session

Notes:

Session Notebook

Date: Start Time: Session No:

Client Name: Session Time:

Topic:

Session Taking Points	Key Points From Previous Session

Notes: _____

_____

_____

_____

_____

_____

_____

_____

_____

_____

_____

_____

_____

_____

_____

_____

_____

_____

Session Notebook

Date: Start Time: Session No:

Client Name: Session Time:

Topic:

Session Taking Points	Key Points From Previous Session

Notes: _____
_____
_____
_____
_____
_____
_____
_____
_____
_____
_____
_____
_____
_____
_____
_____
_____
_____
_____
_____
_____
_____

Session Notebook

Date: _____ Start Time: _____ Session No: _____

Client Name: _____ Session Time: _____

Topic: _____

Session Taking Points	Key Points From Previous Session

Notes: _____

_____

_____

_____

_____

_____

_____

_____

_____

_____

_____

_____

_____

_____

_____

_____

_____

_____

Session Notebook

Date: Start Time: Session No:

Client Name: Session Time:

Topic:

Session Taking Points	Key Points From Previous Session

Notes: _____
_____
_____
_____
_____
_____
_____
_____
_____
_____
_____
_____
_____
_____
_____
_____
_____
_____
_____
_____

Session Notebook

Date: Start Time: Session No:

Client Name: Session Time:

Topic:

Session Taking Points	Key Points From Previous Session

Notes: _____
_____
_____
_____
_____
_____
_____
_____
_____
_____
_____
_____
_____
_____
_____
_____
_____
_____
_____

Session Notebook

Date: Start Time: Session No:

Client Name: Session Time:

Topic:

Session Taking Points	Key Points From Previous Session

Notes: _____

_____

_____

_____

_____

_____

_____

_____

_____

_____

_____

_____

_____

_____

_____

_____

_____

_____

Session Notebook

Date: _____ Start Time: _____ Session No: _____

Client Name: _____ Session Time: _____

Topic: _____

Session Taking Points	Key Points From Previous Session

Notes: _____
_____
_____
_____
_____
_____
_____
_____
_____
_____
_____
_____
_____
_____
_____
_____
_____
_____
_____

Session Notebook

Date: _____   Start Time: _____   Session No: _____

Client Name: _____   Session Time: _____

Topic: _____

Session Taking Points	Key Points From Previous Session

Notes: ————————————————————————————————
_____
_____
_____
_____
_____
_____
_____
_____
_____
_____
_____
_____
_____
_____
_____
_____
_____
_____
_____
_____

Session Notebook

Date: Start Time: Session No:

Client Name: Session Time:

Topic:

Session Taking Points	Key Points From Previous Session

Notes: _____

_____

_____

_____

_____

_____

_____

_____

_____

_____

_____

_____

_____

_____

_____

_____

_____

_____

Session Notebook

Date: Start Time: Session No:

Client Name: Session Time:

Topic:

Session Taking Points	Key Points From Previous Session

Notes: _____

_____

_____

_____

_____

_____

_____

_____

_____

_____

_____

_____

_____

_____

_____

_____

_____

_____

_____

_____

_____

Session Notebook

Date: Start Time: Session No:

Client Name: Session Time:

Topic:

Session Taking Points	Key Points From Previous Session

Notes: _____

_____

_____

_____

_____

_____

_____

_____

_____

_____

_____

_____

_____

_____

_____

_____

_____

_____

Session Notebook

Date: _____ Start Time: _____ Session No: _____

Client Name: _____ Session Time: _____

Topic: _____

Session Taking Points	Key Points From Previous Session

Notes: _____

_____

_____

_____

_____

_____

_____

_____

_____

_____

_____

_____

_____

_____

_____

_____

_____

_____

_____

_____

Session Notebook

Date: Start Time: Session No:

Client Name: Session Time:

Topic:

Session Taking Points	Key Points From Previous Session

Notes:
_____
_____
_____
_____
_____
_____
_____
_____
_____
_____
_____
_____
_____
_____
_____
_____
_____

Session Notebook

Date: _____ Start Time: _____ Session No: _____

Client Name: _____ Session Time: _____

Topic: _____

Session Taking Points	Key Points From Previous Session

Notes: _____

_____

_____

_____

_____

_____

_____

_____

_____

_____

_____

_____

_____

_____

_____

_____

_____

_____

_____

_____

Session Notebook

Date: Start Time: Session No:

Client Name: Session Time:

Topic:

Session Taking Points	Key Points From Previous Session

Notes: _____
_____
_____
_____
_____
_____
_____
_____
_____
_____
_____
_____
_____
_____
_____
_____
_____
_____
_____

Session Notebook

Date: _____   Start Time: _____   Session No: _____

Client Name: _____   Session Time: _____

Topic: _____

Session Taking Points	Key Points From Previous Session

Notes: _____

_____

_____

_____

_____

_____

_____

_____

_____

_____

_____

_____

_____

_____

_____

_____

_____

_____

_____

_____

_____

Session Notebook

Date: Start Time: Session No:

Client Name: Session Time:

Topic:

Session Taking Points	Key Points From Previous Session

Notes:
_____
_____
_____
_____
_____
_____
_____
_____
_____
_____
_____
_____
_____
_____
_____
_____
_____
_____
_____
_____
_____

Session Notebook

Date: Start Time: Session No:

Client Name: Session Time:

Topic:

Session Taking Points	Key Points From Previous Session

Notes: _____

_____

_____

_____

_____

_____

_____

_____

_____

_____

_____

_____

_____

_____

_____

_____

_____

_____

_____

Session Notebook

Date: Start Time: Session No:

Client Name: Session Time:

Topic:

Session Taking Points	Key Points From Previous Session

Notes: _____

_____

_____

_____

_____

_____

_____

_____

_____

_____

_____

_____

_____

_____

_____

_____

_____

_____

Session Notebook

Date: Start Time: Session No:

Client Name: Session Time:

Topic:

Session Taking Points	Key Points From Previous Session

Notes:

Session Notebook

Date: Start Time: Session No:

Client Name: Session Time:

Topic:

Session Taking Points	Key Points From Previous Session

Notes: _____

_____

_____

_____

_____

_____

_____

_____

_____

_____

_____

_____

_____

_____

_____

_____

_____

_____

Session Notebook

Date: _____ Start Time: _____ Session No: _____

Client Name: _____ Session Time: _____

Topic: _____

Session Taking Points	Key Points From Previous Session

Notes: _____
_____
_____
_____
_____
_____
_____
_____
_____
_____
_____
_____
_____
_____
_____
_____
_____
_____
_____

Session Notebook

Date: Start Time: Session No:

Client Name: Session Time:

Topic:

Session Taking Points	Key Points From Previous Session

Notes: _____

_____

_____

_____

_____

_____

_____

_____

_____

_____

_____

_____

_____

_____

_____

_____

_____

_____

Session Notebook

Date: Start Time: Session No:

Client Name: Session Time:

Topic:

Session Taking Points	Key Points From Previous Session

Notes: _____
_____
_____
_____
_____
_____
_____
_____
_____
_____
_____
_____
_____
_____
_____
_____
_____
_____
_____
_____
_____

Session Notebook

Date: Start Time: Session No:

Client Name: Session Time:

Topic:

Session Taking Points	Key Points From Previous Session

Notes: _____
_____
_____
_____
_____
_____
_____
_____
_____
_____
_____
_____
_____
_____
_____
_____
_____
_____

Session Notebook

Date: Start Time: Session No:

Client Name: Session Time:

Topic:

Session Taking Points	Key Points From Previous Session

Notes: _____
_____
_____
_____
_____
_____
_____
_____
_____
_____
_____
_____
_____
_____
_____
_____
_____
_____
_____
_____
_____

Session Notebook

Date: Start Time: Session No:

Client Name: Session Time:

Topic:

Session Taking Points	Key Points From Previous Session

Notes: _____

_____

_____

_____

_____

_____

_____

_____

_____

_____

_____

_____

_____

_____

_____

_____

_____

_____

_____

Session Notebook

Date: Start Time: Session No:

Client Name: Session Time:

Topic:

Session Taking Points	Key Points From Previous Session

Notes:

Session Notebook

Date: Start Time: Session No:

Client Name: Session Time:

Topic:

Session Taking Points	Key Points From Previous Session

Notes: _____

_____

_____

_____

_____

_____

_____

_____

_____

_____

_____

_____

_____

_____

_____

_____

_____

_____

Session Notebook

Date: _____   Start Time: _____   Session No: _____

Client Name: _____   Session Time: _____

Topic: _____

Session Taking Points	Key Points From Previous Session

Notes: _____

_____

_____

_____

_____

_____

_____

_____

_____

_____

_____

_____

_____

_____

_____

_____

_____

_____

_____

Session Notebook

Date: Start Time: Session No:

Client Name: Session Time:

Topic:

Session Taking Points	Key Points From Previous Session

Notes: _____

_____

_____

_____

_____

_____

_____

_____

_____

_____

_____

_____

_____

_____

_____

_____

_____

_____

_____

Session Notebook

Date: Start Time: Session No:

Client Name: Session Time:

Topic:

Session Taking Points	Key Points From Previous Session

Notes: _____
_____
_____
_____
_____
_____
_____
_____
_____
_____
_____
_____
_____
_____
_____
_____
_____
_____
_____
_____

Session Notebook

Date: Start Time: Session No:

Client Name: Session Time:

Topic:

Session Taking Points	Key Points From Previous Session

Notes: _____

_____

_____

_____

_____

_____

_____

_____

_____

_____

_____

_____

_____

_____

_____

_____

_____

_____

_____

Session Notebook

Date: _____   Start Time: _____   Session No: _____

Client Name: _____   Session Time: _____

Topic: _____

Session Taking Points	Key Points From Previous Session

Notes: _____
_____
_____
_____
_____
_____
_____
_____
_____
_____
_____
_____
_____
_____
_____
_____
_____
_____
_____
_____
_____

Session Notebook

Date: Start Time: Session No:

Client Name: Session Time:

Topic:

Session Taking Points	Key Points From Previous Session

Notes: _____

_____

_____

_____

_____

_____

_____

_____

_____

_____

_____

_____

_____

_____

_____

_____

_____

Session Notebook

Date: _____   Start Time: _____   Session No: _____

Client Name: _____   Session Time: _____

Topic: _____

Session Taking Points	Key Points From Previous Session

Notes: _____

_____

_____

_____

_____

_____

_____

_____

_____

_____

_____

_____

_____

_____

_____

_____

_____

_____

_____

_____

_____

Session Notebook

Date: Start Time: Session No:

Client Name: Session Time:

Topic:

Session Taking Points	Key Points From Previous Session

Notes: _____

_____

_____

_____

_____

_____

_____

_____

_____

_____

_____

_____

_____

_____

_____

_____

_____

_____

_____

Session Notebook

Date: Start Time: Session No:

Client Name: Session Time:

Topic:

Session Taking Points	Key Points From Previous Session

Notes: _____

_____

_____

_____

_____

_____

_____

_____

_____

_____

_____

_____

_____

_____

_____

_____

_____

_____

_____

_____

Session Notebook

Date: Start Time: Session No:

Client Name: Session Time:

Topic:

Session Taking Points	Key Points From Previous Session

Notes: _____

_____

_____

_____

_____

_____

_____

_____

_____

_____

_____

_____

_____

_____

_____

_____

_____

_____

_____

Session Notebook

Date: Start Time: Session No:

Client Name: Session Time:

Topic:

Session Taking Points	Key Points From Previous Session

Notes: _____
_____
_____
_____
_____
_____
_____
_____
_____
_____
_____
_____
_____
_____
_____
_____
_____
_____
_____
_____
_____

Session Notebook

Date: Start Time: Session No:

Client Name: Session Time:

Topic:

Session Taking Points	Key Points From Previous Session

Notes: _____

_____

_____

_____

_____

_____

_____

_____

_____

_____

_____

_____

_____

_____

_____

_____

_____

_____

Session Notebook

Date: Start Time: Session No:

Client Name: Session Time:

Topic:

Session Taking Points	Key Points From Previous Session

Notes: _____

_____

_____

_____

_____

_____

_____

_____

_____

_____

_____

_____

_____

_____

_____

_____

_____

_____

_____

_____

Session Notebook

Date: Start Time: Session No:

Client Name: Session Time:

Topic:

Session Taking Points	Key Points From Previous Session

Notes: _____

_____

_____

_____

_____

_____

_____

_____

_____

_____

_____

_____

_____

_____

_____

_____

_____

_____

_____

Session Notebook

Date: Start Time: Session No:

Client Name: Session Time:

Topic:

Session Taking Points	Key Points From Previous Session

Notes: _____

_____

_____

_____

_____

_____

_____

_____

_____

_____

_____

_____

_____

_____

_____

_____

_____

_____

_____

_____

Session Notebook

Date: Start Time: Session No:

Client Name: Session Time:

Topic:

Session Taking Points	Key Points From Previous Session

Notes: _____

_____

_____

_____

_____

_____

_____

_____

_____

_____

_____

_____

_____

_____

_____

_____

_____

_____

_____

_____

_____

Session Notebook

Date: Start Time: Session No:

Client Name: Session Time:

Topic:

Session Taking Points	Key Points From Previous Session

Notes: _____

_____

_____

_____

_____

_____

_____

_____

_____

_____

_____

_____

_____

_____

_____

_____

_____

_____

_____

Session Notebook

Date: Start Time: Session No:

Client Name: Session Time:

Topic:

Session Taking Points	Key Points From Previous Session

Notes:

Session Notebook

Date: **Start Time:**   **Session No:**

Client Name: **Session Time:**

Topic:

Session Taking Points	Key Points From Previous Session

Notes: _____

_____

_____

_____

_____

_____

_____

_____

_____

_____

_____

_____

_____

_____

_____

_____

_____

_____

_____

Session Notebook

Date: Start Time: Session No:

Client Name: Session Time:

Topic:

Session Taking Points	Key Points From Previous Session

Notes: _____

_____

_____

_____

_____

_____

_____

_____

_____

_____

_____

_____

_____

_____

_____

_____

_____

_____

Session Notebook

Date: _____   Start Time: _____   Session No: _____

Client Name: _____   Session Time: _____

Topic: _____

Session Taking Points	Key Points From Previous Session

Notes: _____

_____

_____

_____

_____

_____

_____

_____

_____

_____

_____

_____

_____

_____

_____

_____

_____

_____

_____

_____

_____

Session Notebook

Date: Start Time: Session No:

Client Name: Session Time:

Topic:

Session Taking Points	Key Points From Previous Session

Notes: _____

_____

_____

_____

_____

_____

_____

_____

_____

_____

_____

_____

_____

_____

_____

_____

_____

_____

_____

_____

Session Notebook

Date: Start Time: Session No:

Client Name: Session Time:

Topic:

Session Taking Points	Key Points From Previous Session

Notes: _____

_____

_____

_____

_____

_____

_____

_____

_____

_____

_____

_____

_____

_____

_____

_____

_____

_____

Session Notebook

Date: _____   Start Time: _____   Session No: _____

Client Name: _____   Session Time: _____

Topic: _____

Session Taking Points	Key Points From Previous Session

Notes: _____

_____

_____

_____

_____

_____

_____

_____

_____

_____

_____

_____

_____

_____

_____

_____

_____

_____

_____

_____

Session Notebook

Date: Start Time: Session No:

Client Name: Session Time:

Topic:

Session Taking Points	Key Points From Previous Session

Notes: _____
_____
_____
_____
_____
_____
_____
_____
_____
_____
_____
_____
_____
_____
_____
_____
_____
_____
_____
_____
_____

Session Notebook

Date: Start Time: Session No:

Client Name: Session Time:

Topic:

Session Taking Points	Key Points From Previous Session

Notes: _____

_____

_____

_____

_____

_____

_____

_____

_____

_____

_____

_____

_____

_____

_____

_____

_____

_____

Session Notebook

Date: Start Time: Session No:

Client Name: Session Time:

Topic:

Session Taking Points	Key Points From Previous Session

Notes: _____

_____

_____

_____

_____

_____

_____

_____

_____

_____

_____

_____

_____

_____

_____

_____

_____

_____

_____

_____

_____

Session Notebook

Date: Start Time: Session No:

Client Name: Session Time:

Topic:

Session Taking Points	Key Points From Previous Session

Notes: _____

_____

_____

_____

_____

_____

_____

_____

_____

_____

_____

_____

_____

_____

_____

_____

_____

_____

_____

Session Notebook

Date: _____   Start Time: _____   Session No: _____

Client Name: _____   Session Time: _____

Topic: _____

Session Taking Points	Key Points From Previous Session

Notes: _____
_____
_____
_____
_____
_____
_____
_____
_____
_____
_____
_____
_____
_____
_____
_____
_____
_____
_____
_____

Session Notebook

Date: _____   Start Time: _____   Session No: _____

Client Name: _____   Session Time: _____

Topic: _____

Session Taking Points	Key Points From Previous Session

Notes: _____

_____

_____

_____

_____

_____

_____

_____

_____

_____

_____

_____

_____

_____

_____

_____

_____

Session Notebook

Date: Start Time: Session No:

Client Name: Session Time:

Topic:

Session Taking Points	Key Points From Previous Session

Notes: _____

_____

_____

_____

_____

_____

_____

_____

_____

_____

_____

_____

_____

_____

_____

_____

_____

_____

_____

Session Notebook

Date: Start Time: Session No:

Client Name: Session Time:

Topic:

Session Taking Points	Key Points From Previous Session

Notes: _____

_____

_____

_____

_____

_____

_____

_____

_____

_____

_____

_____

_____

_____

_____

_____

_____

_____

_____

Session Notebook

Date: _____ Start Time: _____ Session No: _____

Client Name: _____ Session Time: _____

Topic: _____

Session Taking Points	Key Points From Previous Session

Notes: _____
_____
_____
_____
_____
_____
_____
_____
_____
_____
_____
_____
_____
_____
_____
_____
_____
_____
_____
_____
_____

Session Notebook

Date: Start Time: Session No:

Client Name: Session Time:

Topic:

Session Taking Points	Key Points From Previous Session

Notes: _____
_____
_____
_____
_____
_____
_____
_____
_____
_____
_____
_____
_____
_____
_____
_____
_____
_____
_____
_____

Session Notebook

Date: Start Time: Session No:

Client Name: Session Time:

Topic:

Session Taking Points	Key Points From Previous Session

Notes: _____

_____

_____

_____

_____

_____

_____

_____

_____

_____

_____

_____

_____

_____

_____

_____

_____

_____

_____

_____

_____

Session Notebook

Date: Start Time: Session No:

Client Name: Session Time:

Topic:

Session Taking Points	Key Points From Previous Session

Notes: _____
_____
_____
_____
_____
_____
_____
_____
_____
_____
_____
_____
_____
_____
_____
_____
_____
_____
_____
_____

Session Notebook

Date: _____   Start Time: _____   Session No: _____

Client Name: _____   Session Time: _____

Topic: _____

Session Taking Points	Key Points From Previous Session

Notes: _____
_____
_____
_____
_____
_____
_____
_____
_____
_____
_____
_____
_____
_____
_____
_____
_____
_____
_____
_____
_____

Session Notebook

Date: Start Time: Session No:

Client Name: Session Time:

Topic:

Session Taking Points	Key Points From Previous Session

Notes: _____

_____

_____

_____

_____

_____

_____

_____

_____

_____

_____

_____

_____

_____

_____

_____

_____

_____

Session Notebook

Date: _____   Start Time: _____   Session No: _____

Client Name: _____   Session Time: _____

Topic: _____

Session Taking Points	Key Points From Previous Session

Notes: _____
_____
_____
_____
_____
_____
_____
_____
_____
_____
_____
_____
_____
_____
_____
_____
_____
_____
_____
_____

Session Notebook

Date: Start Time: Session No:

Client Name: Session Time:

Topic:

Session Taking Points	Key Points From Previous Session

Notes: _____
_____
_____
_____
_____
_____
_____
_____
_____
_____
_____
_____
_____
_____
_____
_____
_____
_____
_____

Session Notebook

Date: Start Time: Session No:

Client Name: Session Time:

Topic:

Session Taking Points	Key Points From Previous Session

Notes: _____
_____
_____
_____
_____
_____
_____
_____
_____
_____
_____
_____
_____
_____
_____
_____
_____
_____
_____
_____
_____

Session Notebook

Date: Start Time: Session No:

Client Name: Session Time:

Topic:

Session Taking Points	Key Points From Previous Session

Notes: _____

_____

_____

_____

_____

_____

_____

_____

_____

_____

_____

_____

_____

_____

_____

_____

_____

_____

_____

Session Notebook

Date: Start Time: Session No:

Client Name: Session Time:

Topic:

Session Taking Points	Key Points From Previous Session

Notes: _____

_____

_____

_____

_____

_____

_____

_____

_____

_____

_____

_____

_____

_____

_____

_____

_____

_____

_____

_____

Session Notebook

Date: Start Time: Session No:

Client Name: Session Time:

Topic:

Session Taking Points	Key Points From Previous Session

Notes: _____

_____

_____

_____

_____

_____

_____

_____

_____

_____

_____

_____

_____

_____

_____

_____

_____

_____

_____

Session Notebook

Date: _____   Start Time: _____   Session No: _____

Client Name: _____   Session Time: _____

Topic: _____

Session Taking Points	Key Points From Previous Session

Notes: _____
_____
_____
_____
_____
_____
_____
_____
_____
_____
_____
_____
_____
_____
_____
_____
_____
_____
_____
_____
_____

Session Notebook

Date: Start Time: Session No:

Client Name: Session Time:

Topic:

Session Taking Points	Key Points From Previous Session

Notes: _____

_____

_____

_____

_____

_____

_____

_____

_____

_____

_____

_____

_____

_____

_____

_____

_____

_____

_____

_____

Session Notebook

Date: Start Time: Session No:

Client Name: Session Time:

Topic:

Session Taking Points	Key Points From Previous Session

Notes: _____
_____
_____
_____
_____
_____
_____
_____
_____
_____
_____
_____
_____
_____
_____
_____
_____
_____
_____
_____
_____

Session Notebook

Date: Start Time: Session No:

Client Name: Session Time:

Topic:

Session Taking Points	Key Points From Previous Session

Notes: _____
_____
_____
_____
_____
_____
_____
_____
_____
_____
_____
_____
_____
_____
_____
_____
_____
_____
_____

Session Notebook

Date: Start Time: Session No:

Client Name: Session Time:

Topic:

Session Taking Points	Key Points From Previous Session

Notes: _____

_____

_____

_____

_____

_____

_____

_____

_____

_____

_____

_____

_____

_____

_____

_____

_____

_____

_____

_____

Session Notebook

Date: Start Time: Session No:

Client Name: Session Time:

Topic:

Session Taking Points	Key Points From Previous Session

Notes: _____

_____

_____

_____

_____

_____

_____

_____

_____

_____

_____

_____

_____

_____

_____

_____

_____

_____

_____

Session Notebook

Date: _____ Start Time: _____ Session No: _____

Client Name: _____ Session Time: _____

Topic: _____

Session Taking Points	Key Points From Previous Session

Notes: _____
_____
_____
_____
_____
_____
_____
_____
_____
_____
_____
_____
_____
_____
_____
_____
_____
_____
_____
_____
_____

Session Notebook

Date: Start Time: Session No:

Client Name: Session Time:

Topic:

Session Taking Points	Key Points From Previous Session

Notes: _____

_____

_____

_____

_____

_____

_____

_____

_____

_____

_____

_____

_____

_____

_____

_____

_____

_____

_____

Session Notebook

Date: Start Time: Session No:

Client Name: Session Time:

Topic:

Session Taking Points	Key Points From Previous Session

Notes: _____

_____

_____

_____

_____

_____

_____

_____

_____

_____

_____

_____

_____

_____

_____

_____

_____

_____

_____

_____

_____

Session Notebook

Date: Start Time: Session No:

Client Name: Session Time:

Topic:

Session Taking Points	Key Points From Previous Session

Notes: _____

_____

_____

_____

_____

_____

_____

_____

_____

_____

_____

_____

_____

_____

_____

_____

_____

_____

_____

_____

Session Notebook

Date: _____   Start Time: _____   Session No: _____

Client Name: _____   Session Time: _____

Topic: _____

Session Taking Points	Key Points From Previous Session

Notes: _____
_____
_____
_____
_____
_____
_____
_____
_____
_____
_____
_____
_____
_____
_____
_____
_____
_____
_____
_____
_____
_____

Session Notebook

Date: _____   Start Time: _____   Session No: _____

Client Name: _____   Session Time: _____

Topic: _____

Session Taking Points	Key Points From Previous Session

Notes: _____

_____

_____

_____

_____

_____

_____

_____

_____

_____

_____

_____

_____

_____

_____

_____

_____

_____

_____

Session Notebook

Date: Start Time: Session No:

Client Name: Session Time:

Topic:

Session Taking Points	Key Points From Previous Session

Notes: _____
_____
_____
_____
_____
_____
_____
_____
_____
_____
_____
_____
_____
_____
_____
_____
_____
_____
_____
_____

Session Notebook

Date: Start Time: Session No:

Client Name: Session Time:

Topic:

Session Taking Points	Key Points From Previous Session

Notes: _____

_____

_____

_____

_____

_____

_____

_____

_____

_____

_____

_____

_____

_____

_____

_____

_____

_____

_____

Session Notebook

Date: Start Time: Session No:

Client Name: Session Time:

Topic:

Session Taking Points	Key Points From Previous Session

Notes: _____

_____

_____

_____

_____

_____

_____

_____

_____

_____

_____

_____

_____

_____

_____

_____

_____

_____

_____

_____

Session Notebook

Date: Start Time: Session No:

Client Name: Session Time:

Topic:

Session Taking Points	Key Points From Previous Session

Notes: _____

_____

_____

_____

_____

_____

_____

_____

_____

_____

_____

_____

_____

_____

_____

_____

_____

Session Notebook

Date: Start Time: Session No:

Client Name: Session Time:

Topic:

Session Taking Points	Key Points From Previous Session

Notes: _____

_____

_____

_____

_____

_____

_____

_____

_____

_____

_____

_____

_____

_____

_____

_____

_____

_____

_____

_____

_____

Session Notebook

Date: Start Time: Session No:

Client Name: Session Time:

Topic:

Session Taking Points	Key Points From Previous Session

Notes: _____

_____

_____

_____

_____

_____

_____

_____

_____

_____

_____

_____

_____

_____

_____

_____

_____

_____

_____

_____

_____

Session Notebook

Date: Start Time: Session No:

Client Name: Session Time:

Topic:

Session Taking Points	Key Points From Previous Session

Notes: _____

_____

_____

_____

_____

_____

_____

_____

_____

_____

_____

_____

_____

_____

_____

_____

_____

_____

_____

_____

Session Notebook

Date: Start Time: Session No:

Client Name: Session Time:

Topic:

Session Taking Points	Key Points From Previous Session

Notes: _____

_____

_____

_____

_____

_____

_____

_____

_____

_____

_____

_____

_____

_____

_____

_____

_____

_____

_____

Session Notebook

Date: Start Time: Session No:

Client Name: Session Time:

Topic:

Session Taking Points	Key Points From Previous Session

Notes: _____

_____

_____

_____

_____

_____

_____

_____

_____

_____

_____

_____

_____

_____

_____

_____

_____

_____

Session Notebook

Date: Start Time: Session No:

Client Name: Session Time:

Topic:

Session Taking Points	Key Points From Previous Session

Notes: _____

_____

_____

_____

_____

_____

_____

_____

_____

_____

_____

_____

_____

_____

_____

_____

_____

_____

_____

_____

Session Notebook

Date: Start Time: Session No:

Client Name: Session Time:

Topic:

Session Taking Points	Key Points From Previous Session

Notes: _____
_____
_____
_____
_____
_____
_____
_____
_____
_____
_____
_____
_____
_____
_____
_____
_____
_____
_____
_____
_____

Session Notebook

Date: Start Time: Session No:

Client Name: Session Time:

Topic:

Session Taking Points	Key Points From Previous Session

Notes: _____
_____
_____
_____
_____
_____
_____
_____
_____
_____
_____
_____
_____
_____
_____
_____
_____
_____
_____

Session Notebook

Date: _____ Start Time: _____ Session No: _____

Client Name: _____ Session Time: _____

Topic: _____

Session Taking Points	Key Points From Previous Session

Notes: _____

_____

_____

_____

_____

_____

_____

_____

_____

_____

_____

_____

_____

_____

_____

_____

_____

_____

_____

_____

_____

_____

Session Notebook

Date: Start Time: Session No:

Client Name: Session Time:

Topic:

Session Taking Points	Key Points From Previous Session

Notes: _____

_____

_____

_____

_____

_____

_____

_____

_____

_____

_____

_____

_____

_____

_____

_____

_____

_____

Session Notebook

Date: _____   Start Time: _____   Session No: _____

Client Name: _____   Session Time: _____

Topic: _____

Session Taking Points	Key Points From Previous Session

Notes: _____

_____

_____

_____

_____

_____

_____

_____

_____

_____

_____

_____

_____

_____

_____

_____

_____

_____

_____

_____

_____

_____

Session Notebook

Date: Start Time: Session No:

Client Name: Session Time:

Topic:

Session Taking Points	Key Points From Previous Session

Notes: _____

_____

_____

_____

_____

_____

_____

_____

_____

_____

_____

_____

_____

_____

_____

_____

_____

_____

Session Notebook

Date: Start Time: Session No:

Client Name: Session Time:

Topic:

Session Taking Points	Key Points From Previous Session

Notes: _____

_____

_____

_____

_____

_____

_____

_____

_____

_____

_____

_____

_____

_____

_____

_____

_____

_____

_____

_____

_____

Session Notebook

Date: Start Time: Session No:

Client Name: Session Time:

Topic:

Session Taking Points	Key Points From Previous Session

Notes: _____
_____
_____
_____
_____
_____
_____
_____
_____
_____
_____
_____
_____
_____
_____
_____
_____

Session Notebook

Date: Start Time: Session No:

Client Name: Session Time:

Topic:

Session Taking Points	Key Points From Previous Session

Notes:

Session Notebook

Date: Start Time: Session No:

Client Name: Session Time:

Topic:

Session Taking Points	Key Points From Previous Session

Notes: _____

_____

_____

_____

_____

_____

_____

_____

_____

_____

_____

_____

_____

_____

_____

_____

_____

_____

_____

Session Notebook

Date: Start Time: Session No:

Client Name: Session Time:

Topic:

Session Taking Points	Key Points From Previous Session

Notes: ————————————————————————————

——————————————————————————————————————
——————————————————————————————————————
——————————————————————————————————————
——————————————————————————————————————
——————————————————————————————————————
——————————————————————————————————————
——————————————————————————————————————
——————————————————————————————————————
——————————————————————————————————————
——————————————————————————————————————
——————————————————————————————————————
——————————————————————————————————————
——————————————————————————————————————
——————————————————————————————————————
——————————————————————————————————————
——————————————————————————————————————
——————————————————————————————————————
——————————————————————————————————————
——————————————————————————————————————

Session Notebook

Date: Start Time: Session No:

Client Name: Session Time:

Topic:

Session Taking Points	Key Points From Previous Session

Notes: _____
_____
_____
_____
_____
_____
_____
_____
_____
_____
_____
_____
_____
_____
_____
_____
_____
_____
_____
_____

Session Notebook

Date: Start Time: Session No:

Client Name: Session Time:

Topic:

Session Taking Points	Key Points From Previous Session

Notes: _____

_____

_____

_____

_____

_____

_____

_____

_____

_____

_____

_____

_____

_____

_____

_____

_____

_____

_____

_____

Session Notebook

Date: Start Time: Session No:

Client Name: Session Time:

Topic:

Session Taking Points	Key Points From Previous Session

Notes: _____

_____

_____

_____

_____

_____

_____

_____

_____

_____

_____

_____

_____

_____

_____

_____

_____

_____

Session Notebook

Date: _____ Start Time: _____ Session No: _____

Client Name: _____ Session Time: _____

Topic: _____

Session Taking Points	Key Points From Previous Session

Notes: ——————————————————————————————

_____

_____

_____

_____

_____

_____

_____

_____

_____

_____

_____

_____

_____

_____

_____

_____

_____

_____

_____

Session Notebook

Date: Start Time: Session No:

Client Name: Session Time:

Topic:

Session Taking Points	Key Points From Previous Session

Notes: _____

_____

_____

_____

_____

_____

_____

_____

_____

_____

_____

_____

_____

_____

_____

_____

_____

_____

_____

_____

Session Notebook

Date: _____   Start Time: _____   Session No: _____

Client Name: _____   Session Time: _____

Topic: _____

Session Taking Points	Key Points From Previous Session

Notes: _____

_____

_____

_____

_____

_____

_____

_____

_____

_____

_____

_____

_____

_____

_____

_____

_____

_____

_____

_____

_____

Session Notebook

Date: _____ Start Time: _____ Session No: _____

Client Name: _____ Session Time: _____

Topic: _____

Session Taking Points	Key Points From Previous Session

Notes: _____

_____

_____

_____

_____

_____

_____

_____

_____

_____

_____

_____

_____

_____

_____

_____

_____

_____

_____

Session Notebook

Date: Start Time: Session No:

Client Name: Session Time:

Topic:

Session Taking Points	Key Points From Previous Session

Notes: _____

_____

_____

_____

_____

_____

_____

_____

_____

_____

_____

_____

_____

_____

_____

_____

_____

_____

_____

Session Notebook

Date: Start Time: Session No:

Client Name: Session Time:

Topic:

Session Taking Points	Key Points From Previous Session

Notes: _____

_____

_____

_____

_____

_____

_____

_____

_____

_____

_____

_____

_____

_____

_____

_____

_____

_____

Made in the USA
Middletown, DE
08 September 2024

60558477R00071